OUR

PURPOSE

IN SPEAKING

OUR
PURPOSE
IN SPEAKING

POEMS BY

WILLIAM

OREM

WHEELBARROW BOOKS ▪ *East Lansing*

♾ The paper used in this publication meets the minimum requirements
of ANSI/NISO z39.48-1992 (R 1997) (Permanence of Paper).

Wheelbarrow Books
Michigan State University Press
East Lansing, Michigan 48823-5245

Printed and bound in the United States of America.

27 26 25 24 23 22 21 20 19 18   1 2 3 4 5 6 7 8 9 10

Library of Congress Control number: 2017957495
ISBN 978-1-61186-290-4 (paper)
ISBN 978-1-60917-571-9 (PDF)
ISBN 978-1-62895-337-4 (ePub)
ISBN 978-1-62896-337-3 (Kindle)

Book design by Charlie Sharp, Sharp Des!gns, East Lansing, Michigan
Cover design by Erin Kirk New
Cover painting of Saint Matthew by Guido Reni (1621)

green Michigan State University Press is a member of the Green
press
INITIATIVE Press Initiative and is committed to developing and
encouraging ecologically responsible publishing practices. For more
information about the Green Press Initiative and the use of recycled
paper in book publishing, please visit *www.greenpressinitiative.org.*

Visit Michigan State University Press at *www.msupress.org*

To my fathers

AUGUSTINE: So you see that our purpose in speaking is solely to teach.

ADEODADTUS: No, that is not clear to me. For if speaking is nothing more than uttering words, I notice that we do that when we sing.

—St. Augustine, *De Magistro*

O my God, what am I
That these late mouths should cry open
In a forest of frost, in a dawn of cornflowers.

—Sylvia Plath, *Poppies in October*

With the publication of William Orem's *Our Purpose in Speaking*, the Residential College in the Arts and Humanities (RCAH) Center for Poetry at Michigan State University continues with our long-dreamed-of project, the Wheelbarrow Books Poetry Series. *Our Purpose in Speaking* is the second book in the series, the first by an emerging author, one who has yet to publish a collection with a major press. We are pleased to introduce William Orem and his work to our readers. Clearly we pay homage to William Carlos Williams and his iconic poem, "The Red Wheelbarrow." Readers will remember the poem begins, "so much depends upon. . . ." that red wheelbarrow. We believe that in the early decades of this twenty-first century, a time when technology, politics, and globalization are changing our lives at a pace we could hardly have imagined, so much depends upon our determination to privilege the voices of our poets, new and old, and to make those voices available to a wide audience. So much depends upon providing a retreat, a place of stillness and contemplation, a place of safety and inspiration. So much depends upon our ability to have access to the words of others so that we see, regardless of race, religion, ethnicity, gender, economic situation, or geographical location, that we all share the human condition, that we are more alike than we are different. Poetry helps us do that. Edward Hirsch reminds us that poetry is one solitude speaking to another—across time, across space, across all of our differences. Audre Lorde reminds us that poetry is not a luxury, it is a necessity. Walt Whitman knew that to have great poets, we must create great audiences. We keep all these things in mind as we continue on with Wheelbarrow Books. So much depends upon the collaboration between our readers and writers, the intimate ways they will come to know one another.

—Anita Skeen, *Wheelbarrow Books Series Editor*

T asked, as I've been, with selecting the one and only, of the handful of manuscripts I've had the pleasure of considering, the one that accomplishes the most of its ambitions, I've read and re-read each of them over the past few weeks, in various orders, different times of the day, in a variety of fettles and focuses. There is much to admire about each of them, and individual poems that will stay with me a good while, but the collection that I found most ambitious and most accomplished, the one without which we would be the most impoverished, is *Our Purpose in Speaking*. In bringing a book of these poems under this title into being, Wheelbarrow Books will be credited with the proper annunciation of an authentic and sinewy voice marked by formal authority, metrical and metaphoric range, imaginative depth, and real intelligence.

I've been honored to judge a fair few first book contests and no winner was more distinctive, more manifestly the best of the bunch, than *Our Purpose in Speaking*. What distinguishes this evocatively titled collection is the comingling of religious literacy, spiritual fluency, and a comfortable apostasy—the result, possibly, of an ambivalent relationship with the dead father (always a stand-in for the gods) that haunts a fair few of these poems, and the learnedness, intelligence, and scholarship that undergirds these astonishing poems. The epigraph to the title poem, from Wallace Stevens's "The Irish Cliffs of Moher" is a clue; likewise, the carnal mysteries, implicit in the fierce closing couplet of the book's last poem, and woven through the entire text. We have at once a manifesto, an examination of conscience, character study, and closing argument for the rich and conflicted internal life the author discloses here in sonnets, sestinas, free verse, and a variety of stanza forms.

"The spiritual life" claimed Meister Eckhart, "isn't so much addition as subtraction."

The same for poetry. *Our Purpose in Speaking* has whittled every extraneous utterance away, leaving the reader that "catch in the breath" Yeats assigned to the apparition of beauty; the hushed tongue of absence and estrangement, the desert's desolation and the body's death, what Heaney called "a silence beyond silence listened for."

A word about the title and its ambitions: In actual fact, I found the title wonderfully evocative, the more so when one regards the author's title poem as a contemplation of the correspondence between a father and son, the author and his absent father. The epigraph to the entire collection, from Augustine's *De Magistro*, whence the title, gives a fuller context by which to understand the poet's regard for language, metaphor, sign, and wonder as elements of instruction, recording, remembrance and re-visioning. The poet sets a high bar by choosing this title, a bar that so many of the poems ably get over. A bit from "A History of Western Philosophy" that illuminates:

2. Augustine on the Teacher. In the De magistro, a dialogue between Augustine and his son Adeodatus, there is a fairly extensive discussion of illumination. The dialogue begins with the fairly innocent question "What are we trying to do when we speak?" The answer, that we are trying to teach or be taught, leads to a discussion of what is happening when we learn something. Augustine prefixes this discussion of the learning process with a long section on words as signs. Although sensible things are incapable of bringing about thought, we make use of words, which are sensible things, presumably to express our thoughts. What effect do words have on the one hearing or seeing them? We might expect Augustine to brush aside the difficulty posed by language as quickly as possible; his actual procedure is quite the opposite, revealing, we may suppose, his former professional interests as a master of rhetoric. The greater part of the dialogue is concerned with words as signs and then with various other kinds of signs.

This, of course, is central to the act of poetry. The addition of the Plath, from "Poppies in October," a poem written on her last, her 30th, birthday, adds a dose of gravitas, and connects to the title poem ("The letters I wrote you at 30"), as does the Wallace Stevens cited in the title poem.

The poet has given us, to misquote Mr. Stevens, "Not only the idea of (his) poetry, but the poetry itself."

Congratulations are due to Wheelbarrow Press on having attracted to its fledgling enterprise, work of such high quality. Publishing poetry, I misquote Don Marquis, "is like casting rose petals into the Grand Canyon and hoping for an echo." This fine first collection echoes fine, rings true, and announces an auspicious debut.

—Thomas Lynch

CONTENTS

OUR PURPOSE IN SPEAKING

CRITICAL

CARE

SONNET: MY MOTHER REFUSES MASTECTOMY

She still believes in Christ, the colored glass,
leaves coins for saints to find her wandered keys.
When we were boys, I'd watch those gifts amassing
at the marble feet of Anthony,
copper on stone. This season, by some art,
the winter sparrows left their berry shreds
in red striations through her snowy yard.
It makes one think of blood—divine, or men's—
one never fully leaves the Catholic dream.
A field of drops on winter snow: a cup:
a cup of bleeding from the whitest fleece.
The hope of worlds beyond this frozen one,

her prayer, at least, for some growth past the suffering.
Outside, all day, the earth dreams of its blossoming.

SNOWFALL EXPECTED AFTER MIDNIGHT

Stepping outside I am struck quite still and dumb by cold
the way nocturnal creatures nestled in the crooks of barns

and hollow boles across the mile-long, empty field must,
I think, be wakened sometimes

by nothing at all,
only the endless, consecutive Sabbath of night—

its deep blue excellence—and the voice,
no voice really, of something just past animal sense:

more a kind of yearning, perhaps, or that flexed sensation
in the hindpart of the ear

when we expect a word, but no word comes, and so
instead
we hear our own listening. How they must go tense

on such nights, field mice furrowed under grass,
chipmunks hid in frosty strips of earth and weed;

or, like the owls with their great soft heads,
all pupil, each retinal cell awakened now to magnify

the heavens' ever-novel blank—exquisite dark—
merely held in cold

suspension;
until they vault into it, each to instinct's end,

the moment passed. Or, possibly,
the moment clutched, its tiny heart mad against the claw;

for this night is knowing nothing
that we do not actually know: simple hunger, simple lust,

nature's ground rules, kill and swallow, cough the bones,
be still, and watch.

MEMORY IS IN OUR FINGERS

With you missing I forget what to do
with my hands. They give me away
shifting constantly and inspecting
    one another
like a pair of lovers.

My hands wander my body
looking for your hands.
They groom, worry. They touch at my face,
    compare it to your face,
find it wanting. Only in sleep

do they come back together. See how
they lie down near me; I wake
to their small
    empty cradle.

THE PHANTOM HITCHER

This road is choked with rain, a slow lament.
You see her formed of

headlight beams, so bright she's half-
                              unseen,

the face an oval hint of blue. Devices
twirl about the clothing: lace?

Or something off a bodice? When
she slips into the bucket seat

the springs don't even crunch.
What else? The radio
is misbehaving (but it always does),
a cigarette you should have hidden

making lines of atmosphere. But she
is home in smoke, sad smile of

that same ephemera, she seems
a creature in-
                    between. And this

is only picking up a girl:
there is no magic any more, no spark

of otherworldly things you once believed.
This is just female flesh beside you now,
gold fingernails and freshly done, a flash
of tragic loveliness. Perhaps

you even smell
the wet night singing in her hair.

⁓

Arriving at the house, of course,
the car is empty,

blank,
as hollow as an eaten gourd.

A witchgrass swatch of earth some dozen yards
beyond the fencing
                holds an unmarked grave.

Imagine knowing decades of rain:
       of disappointed nights,
       of headlights drifting up the hill. Perhaps

this one contains
your freedom, love's

                long-sought deliverance: *this* one; this.

SONNET: *GOLDEN RETRIEVER*
ABANDONED IN FIELD

In finding this, the breath inside you stops
like candlewick between wet fingers. See:
she's young, her black feet scabbed, all four legs wrapped
in tape. Her eyes have brewed two yellow leaks
to salve themselves. Around the snout rude blowflies
strut. *Don't touch it,* someone says, as if these
hurts have made her, too, unclean. But you must try—
you, having felt the hands of men. Who knows
the depth of other minds that share with us
this earth? The injured hip the vet will find, the cuts
both old and fresh, beneath her coat; it's trust
undone, you know, that's worst. And so you sit

quite close to her, ashamed to be afraid.
The tail, with tiny hope, begins to sway.

THE VINEDRESSER

Thorny ground also, if cultivated well, is turned

into fruitful; and is salvation to us irrecoverable?

—Cyril of Jerusalem

It is not the tomatoes, really,
nor the seed-weight that fills their skins,

that solid but tenuous heft—like taking
the first, uncertain time, a woman's breast—

nor is it the kernel of remembered sun
you feel must be nestled in the pith of each.

Something there is just south of a word,
regarding grains of black earth

and the radiant wedges that slip
from the knife to the damp cutting board.

Was it Aquinas who wrote in *The Passions of the Soul*
that to suffer ecstasy is the burden of this world?

Or did I only feel that meaning hidden in his words,
the way a tomato gardener, fingers drifting

among scratchy bundles of leaves
feels instinctively the hanging weight?

We groom the vine,
passing sacks to basket,

red over red, till the heart swims with it.
Afterward, in the sunswept kitchen,

this garden lunch feels like a sacrament.
You and I sit, blessed by such moments,

dazed at such taste,
our muted mouths gleaming their prayer.

∫

STORM SEASON, REHOBOTH BEACH

Belly-up comes the unbelievable wallop
     of sea, its slack mass turned
     to backpedaling slush.
It slips off the beach
        like a dress being dropped.

Streets of no tourist are hazed
with mute cloud. Across town

the wide strap of thunder pulls
like a garter from pink hip
    and slaps.
We stop our dash
        to taste the air,

not knowing what tongue we sought
    or whose flesh.

WOOD, SHELL, STAR

Bay water sways against the failing dock,
a seasonal tide weakening the wood.
This year, the wet joints hold. Some god,
you say, brought forth the Chesapeake with dark hands
and I can see them: palms lapped over endlessly by shells,
a myriad of scattered shapes, like falling stars.

Though science tells us we are made of ancient stars
our lives seem so much closer to this weathered dock:
each day endures its splintering of shells,
each year, the mark of added seasons on the wood.
Ocean water, like insistent hands,
is seeping into what was built by men, not God,

depositing its salt. My love, if I were God
I wouldn't stray so far beyond the stars
when human chores need simple human hands.
We made our Christ a carpenter. This dock,
his soul-strung tree—both sacred wood,
both binding us, like oysters to their shells.

You say: Come hear the sea within the shell,
its presence like a whisper in the house of God.
Across the shoals, the evening wood
begins its choral song; whippoorwills wake under stars.

Night forms around this wooden dock,
a mercy to its creviced hide, ragged like my hands,

which lightly now you take within your softer hands.
Between us we create a hollow, curl of shell:
something unseen, like the dock;
a hidden space, dark as God,
a gift from nowhere, like the stars,
simply there between us, stretched out on this wood.

LOVE POEM (TONIGHT WE SWELL)

Tonight we swell
like bark on tree boles.
Summer dark curls around
street signs, the foolish

picket fence with one rail missing, the man
standing as if strapped
to it all. A small wind

frumps & fusses
like a meddlesome aunt. Sap

blows through the roots to the stems;
you fill me

the way a door

fills its frame

NIGHT FISHING ON CHESAPEAKE BAY

The work they do is fine,
    crafting the waves open with hands
        dipped to the wrist,
            the white forearms slime-crusted.

Purple waves slop and build
    at the boat's ribbed core;
        mucked by some squealing boot
            their prow noses bluntly the swells.

A shore-borne light catches flung brine,
    singing on the silver dross.
        These are dream men, myths,
            fickle with sea break, wending the dark water.

Now comes the trundle of pots,
    hand over hand, spilling froth; the cry of victors,
        sharp as the green ore of nails.
            With a fresh mess of splashes

they achieve: bright jump the fish,
    the broad-mouthed blues,

lean creatures bent to their grasp
in the shape of the risen moon.

SONNET (ONE COMES, THEN, FAINTLY CONSCIOUS)

One comes, then, faintly conscious—as of rain
when one is sleeping late—to life.
The light is clear and true. In later times
such days will smart against your memory's bone.
The Catholic grain was milled after the sheaf,
and graduated you; the Church did clap its stones.
Then childhood rounds its street, and if done well
it knows delight, and how to shape its vowels.
No racks or brands were so but in the head,
where all remembered hurts find echo's wall:
the violence of a drunken home, the halls
that living in was like a martyr's bed.

The daybreak's fresh as when you first began.
We start to live again.

SNAKES IN CEILING

Awareness of their rice paper motion
comes first into your bones,

not your brain: sudden
as a warning chill, the way

you know the words *passed quietly* rest in a letter
one moment before thumbing up the seal.

It is that extra pulse inside a room
to which skin springs alert,

some long-ago evolved instinct for proximity of minds
unlike our own.

~

They are above the dusty ceiling—but only just—
sliding with precision through the hollow eves.
Three, perhaps. It could be more.

The night outside is pitch,
the fields asleep.

    When thought returns, it says

they must have slipped in seeking warmth

or mice, both of which this farmhouse holds
against the changing season.
A fallen roof tile, overhanging trees,
a foot or two of dangling risk,

and in they glide—thin, liquid.

~

I've seen their markings here before
though I'd have thought the autumn killed them off.
In the first, light frost I spied the tracks

come curious 'round the edges of the barn.
Oddly shaped,
spinnings, considerations:

dances, it seemed, in the belly-biting cold.
The largest one (I swear this part

is true) left a perfect question mark
before receding to the grass.

~

It's hard for us, tonight, to turn off all the lights.
We lie in bed upstairs, our genes recalling

all those millennia in mossy dens and caves,
those myths to garden crossers

that always seem to mean more than themselves.
It was like a whisper. No,

like cigarette ash, the sound of burning.
No, caresses in the walls. Will you
make poetry of this?
Midnight has given way

to nothing more than creaking woods,
the long sigh of the poplars.
The roof is theirs, I say, pretending calm,
a biome overhead. Let nature be.

Still, I can't help but picture them,
       our snakes—

       the fishbone ribs, the blinkless eyes—

hanging down in brilliant loops,

slipping through the bedroom lamp,

slung over all our fixtures, in the dark.

ADONAI, ADONAI

> On whom these truths do rest
>
> which we are toiling all our lives to find.
>
> —William Wordsworth, "Intimations of Immortality"

It was always such a grand idea:

a man
who lived among clouds. And not just

clouds, the picture book averred: those crimped-
foil palaces in air,

sunbeam lances

stabbing down
the grass. My God: He

bent the rainbow in his hairy hands, made
Earth dry when it was and

absurdly fecund
when it was,

gave all explanations a resting spot
with his prevenient will.

In fall, leaf-scurry was
his bare feet walking.

Snow landing on snow was his name being whispered.
And later,

when death would come,
or bad sickness, he'd be there,

stroking his antique face
in concern,

telling in the fevered shell of your ear
how *light is from light is from light.*

WITCH CANTICLE

| Aroint.

Down the lane lives a lady who's old as a clock.
Her hair's half-scalp. She sleeps

in a dry canning jar
with a few rotten cores.

Down the lane lives a lady, skin like a shark.
Her kiss is the corn

come up bad, when the worm
spoils the husk

and the farmer pulls a face.
Down the lane lives a lady

who bathes in plum jelly. I believe in her garden
grow fingernail plants.

She has lemons for lunch
dipped in ants.

We went up there one night—
just to see, just for spite.

Out back there's an apple press
doesn't smell right.

The fruit on the floor all have faces
that bite.

In her hands were two boxes: one contains night
with its starlight all clipped into wedges and screws.

The other's a pool
down in deep, if you look,

you can see someone drowning.
It's you, boy. It's you.

JACK O'LANTERNS IN A ROW

How glumly sit these cut-out faces,
brooding over hay arrangements bought at someone's
garden store.

Four golems, cold
                  as a mouthful of earth.

Four words of no
                  consolation. Ominous
quartet.

Their breath—
were each red gourd to exhale,
                even once—

          would be the rain not fallen,
          clay road inaccessible,
          phone line down.

Rook, rook, claw, claw.
Four evangelists sat on a fence

telling the news
        of closet doors
        sliding liquidly open,

of sharp quick willow fingers,
ceiling shadows candle smoke
alarm wires cut, the tool

that reaches past the glass

and pops the window latch.

SONNET: THE WORD *MERCURIAL*

           still brings you back. Thermometer
slipped from your pink wet hand, its fat bulb shattered;
within the silver sink, a deeper silver hovered.
Look, you said, *come see. Come see the mercury.*
Those beads were bright as scissors, quarters from the roll.
I wondered at their taste: would it be bitter fruit?
Or sharp, like fever's tongue? We nosed the drops about
to form weird figures, drawn by startled fingertips:
two men, a house, a nickel-colored heart.
At your behest those ghosts collided, fused, were rent
but always reconvened—until you herded them,
sure Mage, into the sink pipe's all-forgiving throat.

Mercurial. Like father love: now safe, now not,
the dance of the uncertain shapes we built.

ON BEING ASKED, WHILE MAILING POEMS, WHETHER THESE PACKAGES CONTAIN ANYTHING POTENTIALLY HAZARDOUS

O my girl, you can't be sure.
It could be just eruptive. What's in this cool manila may

contain more spunk than Mt Vesuvius, the hook
and thump of Tyson, with more teeth.

There may be wizardry in here
could turn your brain to curds

rend your hohum day beyond
    repair;

one word uniquely forged
or unexpected image sprung

upon you like
a thousand thrashing adders.

      Or perhaps here's gentler stuff,
      some quiet note.

      Perhaps
      to look in here
      you'd balk at simple 3:15

falling cleanly through the afternoon
and resting as it does
upon a violet desk.

A violet desk
beneath a young girl's hand

so lean and easy in its shape.
I mean
this light here,

resting on this very desk; I mean
your
outstretched hand.

THE LOVE GODS ASK

As close as skin
may come
to skin.

She lies in the dripping boughs
      of my torso,

salt rain.
As if not ours these hollows, mouths

seek out each other's shape:

close,

           open,

                  lip, leg.

Bodies
tasting bodies.

           What of their hands, the love gods ask.

We grasp each other
      as if we are falling:
      falling both ways; falling every direction;

falling at once, every part
seeking a grip,
some desperate hold.

What of the tongue?
It finds its nook.

The fingers, then?
Through slippery fields.

The drops? The breaking storm?
Falling every way at once,

each held by the other's holding,
fingers palms

clutch, knot,

now,

just now

just now

comes the rain

SONNET: CAPITOL HILL, 1981

A desperate wind blew through the homeless men
where I was young. *You must in them*
see God, the Jesuits explained, *as in the mugger, Christ.*
The phrase fixed in my brain. *The mugger Christ*
came at me with a switchblade grin; he took
my watch and wallet, stooping
in a dry-dock, tossing dice. *The mugger Christ.* At night

we snuck out to the trestle rails, far from the city's frights:
safe in that dark we'd leap from steel to steel
and dance upon the ties, shout out the names of cargo cars
and, fearless now, release our souls to flight
beneath a caterwaul of stars

(but every line was driven by the Christ
 his eye a spinning wheel)

CRITICAL CARE

"This," I answered, "must be as it may please
heaven, but tell me and tell me true, I see my poor
mother's ghost close by us; she is sitting by the
blood without saying a word, and though I am her
own son she does not remember me and speak to
me; tell me, Sir, how I can make her know me."

I don't see him that Autumn, my father, and then
it is too late. The chance is not given
to hand back the anger
that was my daily angel, growing and surviving in his

house. Instead,

I live the process of this,
my mother's slower passing:
gathering pieces of it,
those that are my own.

~

Hospital gleam, the terrible kindness of staff,
some lemony tea.
Talk of this time in her life as *transition*
rather than *terminus,* one rocky gap
past which arboreal comforts lie.

Mid-sentence, she sleeps.
I think the far-too-chipper priest
who moves from bed to bed with what he has brought
was once a young man with parent issues of his own;

I worry that no one cradles the dead,
that God was a word
not just in the Beginning, but also the end.

～

Here is a prayer for my father who struck me with his
open hand:
at peaceful tables may he find
　　　　the staple of love's good bread.

Here is a prayer for my mother who drank badly,

　　　　who stole my mail out of the slot
　　　　to keep away other women,
　　　　who called me *wicked* and *rotten* and *shame*,
　　　　who was my first model of love,
　　　　who drank until her eyes were gray jelly,
　　　　whose refrain was *you just don't care*
　　　　and *you think you're so damned clever*
　　　　who drank herself to the rug

from whom I hid in the basement, under the bed,
in the hall closet
behind the hanging coats and boots,
smelling wool, hearing the sound of her blackeyed
rages:

may she receive in heaven's bower
all her gentle portion.

When she wakes, it takes some time to understand who I am.
She is sitting by the blood without saying a word. Carefully,
I take her cool, too-soft palm,
feeling the bones.

This is us, then,
my hated mother and I;

these is how our together ends.
See how in one hand we hold each other
while in the other we hold out our hearts.

Don't go yet:

don't make the journey five, ten years into the future
when all this will just be poetry.

Stay a little, in this little yellow room;
just a bit more

with the tea and the bad son
and the young priest who has drawn up a chair now,
full of inaccessible smiles.

Try to understand.

This is my mother;
these are my best reassurances to her;
this is the way we speak

as if we had found consolation,
as if the narrow cracker between tongue
and palate were, in fact, a door.

OUR

PURPOSE

IN SPEAKING

SONNET: FRANCIS TO THE BIRDS

In time, they'll say I came to teach you songs of mine:
a canticle of suffering, and tears
around a thorny head in Palestine.
You birds, it is not so. I come to hear.
Grant me whatever grace is there inside your breasts
and drives the happy life from which you grow.
Grant me the blue heart tapping in the sheltered nest,
the subtle flutes and filters of your bones.
With broken sighs my brothers march their broken way;
with lamentation, take to dirty knees.
But I myself shall bow this day
among the tents of feathered ministry,

for I have found you crying hopeful airs
superior to prayer. You birds, I come to hear.

FIFTY-FOUR ACRES

Just as twilight grows thick enough to feel it
deer emerge in the unplowed field.

We are strangers to this landscape, to the intuitions
    farmers know,
the practicalities of soil, the drudge and spit
    of labor.
We're in this house as guests, and miles from town.

Now in gradual blue the mother tilts,
    her eyes form twin dollops.
She seems to be showing them how to drink the Earth—
    her fawns, her two quick fawns.

Their necks are brown as antique paper.
You'd touch the noses if you could:
    an unshelled snail, moss underneath a creek.

All three dance in the sunlight's branches
    and are gone,
and I think how the world leaps daily to find itself,

over and over, finding itself.

THE SWIMMER

I.

In early wintertime she drove there (he had left her then),
crossed by ferry,
                        arrived at mothy dusk.
Alone now in the blackly drafted house
she lay before the fireplace

wrapped in an afghan
cold but alive.

II.

All that night
strange constellations wheeled
through empty window frames.

Upstairs she found the old brass bed
just as it had been:
a heavy counterpane
from her mother's generation.
At dawn she slept,
                        feeling the house shift

        and snap,
the rafters dream.

III.

She stayed the weekend, then the week.
Drove to the local market at most need,

eggs brown and weighty; sugar dark,
bacon wrapped in paper
by the inquisitive grocer's hands.
Would she be rooming up there long?
Sometimes she wandered miles by foot

through sleeping gardens,
hills in the late season.
Chill wind trembled inland

off the mighty lake,
a question.

IV.

That morning when she heard the cry
she rose from oatmeal and,
bare-legged, clutching at her ribs,
hurried down the flagstones.
How could she say the thing she saw?

Brightly backed by sun, its sides crashing down gray
water,

an elk,
snout jutted high for air;
she had not known their kind could swim.

From where was it arriving? And what
had summoned such a hulk of life
to these spent waters, this
remorseless coast?

It rose, the huge

V.

machinery of legs still streaming, staggered in the weeds,
muscles fierce and slick.
She saw the rude mist steaming off its flanks,
the nostrils' ragged cloud.

A second time it made its cry—a bellow,
trumpeting,
a song of lived transition.
And she joined in (Should not

all triumph sing?)—
two victors by the blowing waves

shouts bearing each forward.

AT SUMMER'S END WE CAME
TO THE DARKENING SEA

At summer's end we came to the darkening sea. I entered it
as I once entered you, not knowing either;

taking the waves' cold insistence to my core, skin thickening
with each abrasion. Beachfront Delaware

was decked out in its finery of sharp
      shell pieces,
keels and sea glass. O my drowning one

how far did we travel, that day, on that rain-speckled face—
what breakers passed,

what ruined masts, around our feet always
the white churn hurrying?

The shoreborne gusts embraced us in their salty whips.
Hard blew the desperate life

of you and I, the ships.

I WANT THE LIGHT NO ONE SEES

I want the light no one sees,
wastefully draped across ten thousand

tangled branches through all
open unhoused country.

I want the moons that shone before men
saw moons shining;

their blue talc lining miles of footless sand.
I want the rose

that lay along these harbor towns
when everyone was sleeping

who might have said: how grand. I want the light
whose failing edge my father saw

that morning when he stopped
between the dining room and den,

and, without violence, sound
or any final thing,

simply lay down there
for us to find,

a man of shadows, keeper
of what is not lit.

METAPHOR OF THE CAVE

Darkness curls in deft slopes
around these tongues.

They are dancing figures,
       the fire in twin caves.
They are bodies seeking each other

for substance.
So tremulous,
       quavering in and out of shape

the taking and lending of forms
in the saltwet scoop of the kiss,

in the place
       of true union.

CHRISTMAS EVE, NORTH
OF DOLAN, INDIANA

I hear the impact, glass over asphalt,
the pickup engine's warm growl.
At the edge of the field
between snow piles she is lying,

head bent on exposed grass,
the grit nose still testing for scents.
The ice where she skidded has blood—

not the Hollywood way, full
of drama; only dirty ribbons of stuff
losing oxygen fast in the black
     midnight air.

At the house I phone Animal Control,
go back to crouch near the quivering body.
If I prayed, it was for confusion and softness in her brain,
not the frightful awareness of endings,
that human knowledge,
nor the animal's immediacy of pain.

After long minutes, the sheriff's van slows to a purr
bathing her hot flanks in red.
A slick road,
          a doe,

                a brake pedal missed:
small effort is made for such things.

With the gun out
he leans over her belly,
away from the feet, which may kick.
And I want to say something, some word about flesh
and the waiting cross; childhood stories

of Christ our Lord
and the animals who knelt down
on this night.

        ~

The act we commit
brings an echo, then nothing—no following sigh

from the deep winter trees, from the hillsides
asleep in their swaddling of white.

SONNET: THE DREAM UNDOES
ITS EXPOSITION

The dream undoes its exposition, idling
off. That other, conscious, life
again begins. It seems we're always re-arriving
here: the common world, our waking up.
How odd to rise to history—the much,
                    the all who ever were—
and merely crack a paper by a shining cup.
Or do you still prefer

those best-of times when, in a regular amaze,
we choose to drift an hour, like saints
still in their beds and addle-brained
                    by unexpected joy? In either case

the grass slopes off its morning dew.
One starts, once more, the unconcluded work of being new.

OUR PURPOSE IN SPEAKING

> My father's father, his father's father, his—
> Shadows like winds
>
> Go back to a parent before thought, before speech…
> —*Wallace Stevens, "The Irish Cliffs of Moher"*

The letters I wrote you at 30
you marked *Return to Sender*. I had learned to speak then,

to ask if the hurt man slung to the church wall was real,
to question the stories you told of Korean soldiers

mounting gray hills in impossible waves: that sound
you described of a thousand mouths shrieking.

Saints have called true speech unreachable,
words merely gestures:
        said we only lean toward the truth

like coleus in September fields
        yearning at the sun,

naive but expectant
as children.

∫

The Desert Fathers, too, leaned into fortnights of prayer,
blackening their fingertips on papyrus,
rubbing the words, as if to wear from them

the housing that seemed always
to conceal what it named; or as if
by such staining

to make of themselves
a novel addendum to the divine
elocution.

For a time I was Aquinas,
flinging my sheets to an indifferent noon. *All I have written,*

the saint once wrote, *seemed to me like straw.*
Had I loaded those letters home

with jasmine and honey
you'd have rendered them voiceless the same—

ink cast in traveling water,
a darkening briefly, blood from a cut.
And then the old numbness, the cold
clear stream.

Dear Father:

At age twelve you drove us to St. Michael's Town
to nestle for a season in an oysterman's cottage.
The shore grass clustered
       higher than my brow,
thick near the whisper of reeds
their heads bobbed with the plumb weight of
            crickets.
I loved you then fiercer than any other time.
In the changing twilight

       bats dropped from their branches
snapping bugs off the cool lip of the Bay.
You laughed and lied, calling them birds,
you and I floating
       in trembling black

two human shapes cast among stars.

No, here *I* lie:
it was my brother who said they were birds
to comfort my fear;
he who swam that night at my side;
you were not there. I have no clear

memory of you,
then or any time,
only the carved outline of your absence
that followed me always, the way the cross
is said to have followed young Jesus

so that even when he was playing in the mud
        after a rain,
or pulling on his fingers,
pretending to be Achilles or Moses,

still something was there, bothering him,
something always, an absence,
an absence that defined him,
a shadow that defined his life, every morning when
he awakened.

WHALE, CAPE HENLOPEN

By afternoon the sky was sooty, looming
     rain.
The broad Atlantic blew and turned
     and blew again.

And here it lay,

    slung up by some green wave
        and muttered over by approving crabs.

The meat was cleaned but recent.
          Living bone,

still pliant blue. A outraged mess
of gulls
     exploded off the glistering sand.

We still could see

    the gentle rest of hip in spine,
    a treasury of scattered vertebrae.

And something of the jaw, wherein
    they say the music lies—

that long, expressive arc,

like us, that sings.

"GREAT NATURE HAS ANOTHER THING TO DO TO YOU AND ME"

> When historians sought to exhume the bones of
> colonist Roger Williams, they found that roots of
> a nearby apple tree had consumed the calcium in
> his bones and formed a pattern of living tissue that
> mimicked his skeleton.
>
> —William Dietrich, *Our Northwest*

This is the final reduction of men:
from hard accomplishment, sweat labor done,
wisdom and the far field planted,

down to a prodding root—
its curious tip nudging skull, clavicle,
the spent lunate
beneath which, once, such manful spirits leapt.

The sip

of one determined stem
and *we shall be transformed*:

men who in their time were rugged towers,
men who quoted Job against insistent drizzle,
men whose days were flinging plow to muck
for thick ideals,

those who heard the stern gulls' cry
and filled the pilot's seat; and down before their feet

fell these: a hundred elms,
a thousand elders, ripped like Caesar was from mother's
clay,

the root-balls loosed with rope
and bodily displayed, like vanquished foes,
in cataracts of raining, ruined earth.

The trees, in turn,
are patient in their years.

They have not man's bright ax
      nor flame.

They bring, in time,
what all of nature brings:

          simple
          inquisitiveness, a touching.

SONNET: LUST

Inside me, low, there sits a sullen ache.
Be not mistaken in its cause: it's LUST.
I'll not put words between two bucking facts:
the world is old enough for *tongue across her salty bust*
and always was. All that it speaks to me today
is you, this low insistence; all that it knows
is two: wings and the flying time. *My sun! My bliss!*
is silly words, mere poets' hocus-pocus,
much mooning over conquests lost and won.
But straightly toward you now, my own,
one thought with focus

             runs:

do you come home, and bring no wasteful roses.
I long to hear your sudden frantic *O yes*

SONNET: AFTER THE CREMATORIUM

At ten, I touched a finger to a white stove ring
to see if pain would come.
So much of what you told me was a lie.
Father, there is no resurrection by a shining King;
your body ash we poured into the brackish
Chesapeake. I saw that morning's tide
transport you out to rippled nothingness,
your form as gossamer as Spring, the brow
whose fury, once, had fumed and frighted all our house.
The day we let you go was calm. The world
wherein the only love that ever truly was takes place
surrounded us, and bore you down. And now

your shadow's length, I find, lies nowhere on my floor.
How shall I lie? To claim our dissolution had not started
long before?

CATECHUMEN

What did the old Cistercian say
regarding heaven when you spoke?

      That there will come
      some tutelage of mercy,
      the brightening signs of which

      perceived, for now,
      in part
      may hold one's trust.

What did he say
of heaven's like?

      That each vase in the cupboard
      may be filled up to its edge;

      so that,
      in just this way,
      the crowd of souls shall each
      have more or less, depending
      on our inner shape.

And what was said that day
  of hell?

That it is

self-made loneliness, a choosing
to be far.

And what had you
to offer back?

All that I know:

that wide awake inside the man
awaits the child he will become

IN MEMORIAM ERWIN SCHROEDINGER, AUGUST 1887–JANUARY 1961

What she didn't understand—being a tabby
and unacquainted with loss and how it shapes itself

quietly around the contours of our lives
sometimes almost comforting

with its soft familiarity—
was how, when I lifted the attic box

(it was well past time to clean up there) and,
from inside, the belled collar gave its little chime

so that she came running, happily if cats do show happiness,
expecting her companion to emerge

as if the tom had just been left, somehow,
all those months ago, in the upstairs room:

he who had been carried out, old friend,
his yellow head exhausted on my elbow's crook

the fur on him all spiky and bad-smelling
and simply not been seen by her again—

what she could not understand, I mean to say,
though she rubbed fiercely the cardboard fringe

wet-nosing and rummaging the corners,
was that there was no one inside:

not a bit of her playmate,
littermate, sole feline partner of eleven years.

It was just a noisy collar which, at the last moment,
her ridiculous owner had been unable to toss

and so had done the human thing:
tucking it away, gone without having to admit it,

without goodbye or not-goodbye.
No work then to do then, I suppose. No puzzles,

no questions we with our puffed-up simian brains
and all our tricks and powers still can't scan.

How there can be a common cardboard box,
brown,

corrugated,
that both does and does not have everything in it at once.

HANDMAIDEN

For this meditation, let us think on *Miryam-bat-Joachim*,
called Mary, called
           the virginal,

twelve or thirteen years at most, tangled
hair concealed   skin

                    the color of Ottoman coffee, eyes
                    already trained in looking down.

A face

clean as wheat, dark as thunder
when crossed (all girls are)
holding its own secret life (all girls are).

Mary, *Miryam*,
legs like cinnamon

bathing with your sisters in the public stream

breasts like almond skins: the angel
placed a finger on your womb

and said: here is my text.

∫

       ~

                        Was God a fair lover

      Miryam

moving in shadows
behind the dappled sky?
Blushing like blood

        in evening clouds

Tell us, o Lady,
how spirit enters flesh to
the experience of man;

tell us of that moment where

        such dumb beasts as we are can meet
        such speaking souls as we may be

  ~

You felt

something enter you like a man
I saw one like a son of man
something quite up past your thighs

passing into you over you the wings undid your sight
suspended you from threads
sun and moon, star and womb

and someone's groaning shadow—

come under my roof,
come under my roof

Mary

Mary

My Lord, you have eclipsed me

EPITAPH FOR UNWRITTEN POETRY

Because it was late, and tomorrow
        was a work day,
          and unwashed dishes sulked on the counter,

I tucked you under notebook covers
like children to bed,
saying I loved you and would return,
            knowing it was lies, lies.

Or because others papers needed their attending—
        glossy windowed envelopes
         that grimaced with authority; or because

swarms of pixels distracted me,
night and day
with their assaultive hive.

Or perhaps I simply didn't feel like it—
            did not feel the new life to come
(you don't know what sharp sticking pain it
 sometimes is)
            would be worth the labor of its
raising; or then

because I was fatigued anxious self-satisfied my bones
full of

ashes and shadows
and the sounds of voices
I already did not wish to hear.

The truth is, I was afraid:
I was just so damn afraid.

Often of what you'd say—sometimes of what you wouldn't—
afraid of what might follow
were I to take the time,
sit—with paper, pen—

sit, in appropriate silence paused—

    and say:

        Now.
        I hear you.
        I want you.

        Go ahead: speak.

JALOUSIE MALADIVE

I built a birdhouse for my summer love
and found her with another summer man.
Fly up, my birds, I said, *and pluck his eyes.*

Fill in their hollow shells with seed and cover
the blanks that only perching sorrow can;
I built a birdhouse for my summer love.

Like torrent water grew my summoned flock
around me swelling in a feathered dance.
Fly up, my birds, I said, *and pluck his eyes.*

Where thinning air grew perilous with sun
and silver flight looked down on beaten strands
I built a birdhouse for my summer love.

My blight I fed 'til curse and man were one;
my curse I coughed out on that blasted land:
(Fly up, my birds, I said, *and pluck his eyes)*—

*"Anoint with wax my flightless skin and tell
each tendon to receive the feathered lash."*

I built a birdhouse for my summer love.
Fly up, my birds, I said, *and pluck his eyes.*

TIDEWATER

for Richard Hoffman

It is past midnight, deep

into the time when our spouses sleep
and we see ourselves

        as children, as we are.

Blue arcs lance through silent sky.
I am below, an animal that dies.

Human bond I have thought scattered shells, too fragile
to persist.
Above us, through chaotic fronds,

this lightless canopy of sound.
Beneath, where all men lie, relentless mist.

NEW YEAR'S DAY (HERE IS YOUR MORNING SKY)

Here is your morning sky the color of sleep
this is the loom where God spreads you

this is the bright sound of stones
beneath a crumbling wind;

these are the rooks that crowd the winter air with exaltation
rising like a black wave
on a black sea

what is that moment wherein we stand naked before
all that is yet to become

before every hour and thing
reaching up toward now

if not the promise of holiness,
if not the coming of the Lord?

THE WOMAN UPSTAIRS MAKING LOVE

Now I know the sound of your welcome:
now I know your patience,

your slowness taking in,
your motion in return,

the acceptance, forgiveness,
the forgiveness even of need.

There is no hissing or chatter of bedsprings,
no noise like fighters

that struggle but do not witness
the deliberateness of love.

I know only bodies
dropped to a mattress, hands on the warm rises

and wells of the spine. In the peak
is the seed of its finish:

already, it closes.
And now you must lie wrapped

in drifting—that sweet
after-joy of the loins,

the luminous roused breathing, lips
that have sounded the cry

I heard,
and that I too am sounding,

here, beneath you,
unknown, but with you.

SONNET: CRUCIFIX

Stretched out in alabaster, now they see
this supple-muscled man. A plastercast display
of Medieval pains fixed to a nave.
Blue wires and crumbled paint. It's lovely, in the way
cadavers sometimes are: vein-marbled knees
and bone-struck feet, the wincing simple face,
the painted hair. A thousand pricks of bees
adorn his flanks, and he adorns a star-filled space.
I used to wonder what the artist felt
detailing this sad state with bristle touch,
devoting patient hours to it; how he must have knelt
and whispered to his god, *help me depict your love—*

and then, each night, before the mirror, stood and gazed,
as if not once before, at something living, strange—

ACKNOWLEDGMENTS

"*Adonai, Adonai,*" *The Rockhurst Review*

"Catechumen," "Wood, Shell, Star," "Sonnet: Francis to the
Birds," *Rock & Sling*

"Christmas Eve, North of Dolan, Indiana," *Grub Street Free
Press*

"Fifty-four Acres," *Best Poem: A Literary Journal*

"Great nature has another thing to do to you and me," *Caesura*

"Jack o'Lanterns in a Row," *Glassworks Magazine*

"*Jalousie Maladive,*" *Harbinger Asylum*

"Storm Season, Rehoboth Beach," *KYEzine*

"Love Poem (Tonight We Swell)," *Erotic Readers and Writers
Association*

"Memory Is in Our Fingers," *Runes: A Review of Poetry*

"Metaphor of the Cave," *Princeton Arts Review*

"Night Fishing on Chesapeake Bay," *Midwest Review*

"On Being Asked, While Mailing Poems, Whether These
Packages Contain Anything Potentially Hazardous," *The
New Verse News*

"Snowfall Expected after Midnight," "Snakes in Ceiling,"
"Critical Care," "The Vinedresser," *Nimrod*

"Sonnet: My Mother Refuses Mastectomy," *Writings on the
Body*

"Sonnet: After the Crematorium," "Sonnet: Capitol Hill, 1981,"
The New Formalist

"Sonnet: Crucifix," "Sonnet: *Golden Retriever Abandoned in
Field,*" *Open Poetry International*

"Sonnet: The Word *Mercurial*," *Alehouse*

"The Love Gods Ask," *Tupelo Press*

"The Phantom Hitcher," *Dogwood*

"The Swimmer," *Raleigh Review*

"The Woman Upstairs Making Love," *Penware Poetry Awards*

"Whale, Cape Henlopen," *Color Wheel*

"Witch Canticle," *Perfume River*